W9-CYD-243

Juvenile

DISASTER ALERT!

HURRICANE AND TYPHOON ALERT!

Revised and Updated Edition

Paul Challen

Crabtree Publishing Company
www.crabtreebooks.com

For Sam, Evelina, and Henry

Researcher and editor: Adrianna Morganelli

Proofreader: Emily McMullen

Photo research: Crystal Sikkens

Cover design: Ken Wright

Editorial director: Kathy Middleton

Print coordinator: Katherine Berti

Prepress technicians: Margaret Amy Salter and Ken Wright

First edition:
    Coordinating editor: Ellen Rodger
    Project editor: Sean Charlebois
    Copy editor: Carrie Gleason
    Proofreader: Adrianna Morganelli
    Designer and production coordinator: Rosie Gowsell
    Art director: Rob MacGregor
    Photo research: Allison Napier
    Indexer: Wendy Scavuzzo

Consultant: Dr. Richard Cheel, Earth Sciences Department, Brock University

Cover: Large boats carried by the powerful winds of Hurricane Katrina were dropped on a road in southern Louisiana, U.S.A.
Contents: Hurricanes bring powerful winds and heavy rain.
Title page: Winds from Hurricane Wilma strike southern Florida, U.S.A., on October 25, 2005.

Photographs:
American Red Cross: Daniel Cima: page 4
Associated Press: pages 19 (bottom), 22, 23 (top)
Archives Charmet/Bridgeman Art Library: page 5
FEMA: Jocelyn Augustino: cover (bottom); Melissa Ann Janssen: page 16 (top); Jacinta Quesada: page 19 (top); Robert Kaufmann: page 23 (bottom); Red Cross: page 25 (middle right); Andrea Booher: page 27; Greg Henshall: page 29 (top)
National Oceanic and Atmospheric Administration/Department of Commerce: pages 11 (top right), 14, 17 (bottom), 20 (bottom), 25 (top)
Photo Researchers Inc.: Will & Deni McIntyre: page 28
Shutterstock: pages 3, 8, 20 (top), 24, 25 (top left and bottom right), 26
Visuals Unlimited: Marc Epstein: page 1
Weatherstock/Warren Faidley: page 21
Wikipedia: Jeff Schmaltz, MODIS Rapid Response Team, NASA/GSFC: cover (top); NOAA: pages 6, 15, 18; TAFB/NHC/NOAA: page 16 (bottom); NASA: page 17 (top); Ignis: page 29 (bottom)

Illustrations:
Dan Pressman: pages 9, 10, 11 (bottom left and right), 12-13, 13 (bottom)
David Wysotski, Allure Illustrations: pages 30-31

Map:
Jim Chernishenko: page 7

Library and Archives Canada Cataloguing in Publication

Challen, Paul, 1967-
    Hurricane and typhoon alert! / Paul Challen. -- Rev. ed.

(Disaster alert!)
Includes index.
Issued also in electronic format.
ISBN 978-0-7787-1593-1 (bound).--ISBN 978-0-7787-1626-6 (pbk.)

    1. Hurricanes--Juvenile literature. 2. Typhoons--Juvenile literature.
I. Title. II. Series: Disaster alert!

QC944.2.C45 2011   j551.55'2   C2010-907574-9

Library of Congress Cataloging-in-Publication Data

CIP available at Library of Congress

Crabtree Publishing Company

www.crabtreebooks.com   1-800-387-7650

Printed in China/022011/RG20101116

Published in Canada
Crabtree Publishing
616 Welland Ave.
St. Catharines, Ontario
L2M 5V6

Published in the United States
Crabtree Publishing
PMB 59051
350 Fifth Avenue, 59th Floor
New York, New York 10118

Published in the United Kingdom
Crabtree Publishing
Maritime House
Basin Road North, Hove
BN41 1WR

Published in Australia
Crabtree Publishing
386 Mt. Alexander Rd.
Ascot Vale (Melbourne)
VIC 3032

Table of Contents

Wild Whirlwinds

Hurricanes are large, spiral-shaped storms with very strong winds. Every year, dozens of these powerful storms travel thousands of miles across warm ocean waters, unleashing heavy rain and high waves along the way. Hurricanes usually remain out at sea where they do little damage, but some reach land. When a hurricane strikes land, its violent winds and surging ocean waters threaten lives and cause billions of dollars in damage to coastal properties.

Wind and waves from Hurricane Alex lash the coast of Corpus Christi, Texas, as it comes ashore.

What is a disaster? A disaster is a destructive event that affects the natural world and human communities. Some disasters are predictable and others occur without warning. Coping successfully with a disaster depends on a community's preparation.

Corpus Christi, Texas

Explaining hurricanes

Weather scientists, called **meteorologists**, know much more about hurricanes today than they did just a few years ago. Advances in technology have allowed meteorologists to forecast, or predict, the strength, path, and duration of hurricanes with better accuracy. This information is used to give warning to people in danger so they can protect themselves and their property during a hurricane. Forecasting methods have saved many lives, but they have not made hurricanes any less dangerous. Each year these devastating storms claim lives all over the world.

Early beliefs

Hundreds of years ago, people who lived in parts of the world where hurricanes are common believed these terrible storms happened because they had angered gods that controlled nature. In Central America, the Mayan people believed that their god Hunraken, whipped up tremendous winds at will, often with disastrous effects. The Taino people of Haiti, Puerto Rico, and the South American country of Venezuela, had a similar spirit, known as Jurakán, who was considered an evil god because of his ability to create powerful and sometimes deadly storms. In Australia, coastal Aboriginal people believed that a spirit called Nungalinya, or "Old Man Rock," caused hurricanes and earthquakes when he was angry.

(above) In this illustration from the 1800s, a Paraguas shaman in the South American country of Paraguay, attempts to turn away an approaching hurricane by using magic.

Spinning Storms

Hurricanes are cyclonic storms, which means they rotate, or spin, around a calm center called an eye. Where a cyclonic storm originates determines whether it is called a hurricane, a typhoon, or a tropical cyclone. Even though they are called by three different names, these storms are exactly the same.

What's in a name?

In North, South, and Central America, cyclonic storms are called hurricanes. In the western Pacific Ocean and the China Sea, people call these storms typhoons. The word "typhoon" comes from the Greek word for "whirlwind." The Chinese called typhoons "tai fung" which means "big wind." In the Indian Ocean and the southwest part of the Pacific Ocean, these storms are known as tropical cyclones, or simply as cyclones. In Australia, they are called by the Aboriginal phrase "willy willies," while in the Philippines, they are called *bagios*.

The calm center eye can clearly be seen in this satellite image of Hurricane Katrina.

Winds of change

A hurricane, typhoon, or cyclone must have winds that exceed speeds of 74 miles per hour (119 km/h), and these wind speeds must last for ten minutes or more.

'Tis the season

There are four main regions where cyclonic storms form in the world's oceans. Each region's storms develop in different seasons, when weather conditions are just right in that part of the world. In the Atlantic Ocean, hurricane season lasts from June to December. North Pacific typhoons occur between June and October. In the southern part of the Pacific, cyclone season takes place between January and March. Cyclones in the Northern Indian Ocean occur between June and November.

Cyclonic storms occur only in the tropical regions of the world just above and below the equator. Many Atlantic hurricanes form off the west coast of Africa, about 1,000 miles (1,600 km) from the Cape Verde Islands. These storms are known as Cape Verde hurricanes and follow a westerly route, usually late in the season. Cape Verde hurricanes are usually very powerful because they gain strength traveling long distances across the ocean. Hurricanes do not form right at the equator or in the South Atlantic Ocean.

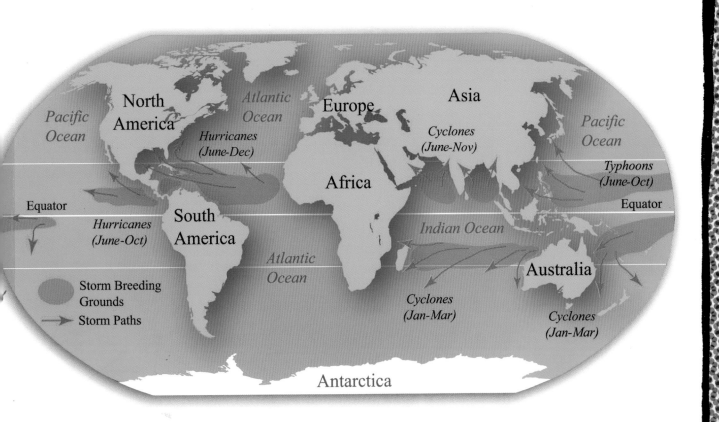

North America

Pacific Ocean

Atlantic Ocean

Europe

Asia

Pacific Ocean

Hurricanes (June-Dec)

Cyclones (June-Nov)

Typhoons (June-Oct)

Equator

Equator

Hurricanes (June-Oct)

South America

Africa

Indian Ocean

Atlantic Ocean

Australia

Storm Breeding Grounds

Storm Paths

Cyclones (Jan-Mar)

Cyclones (Jan-Mar)

Antarctica

How Hurricanes Form

Every year, hundreds of storms form over the tropical portions of the Earth's oceans. Only a small number of these storms become hurricanes. In order for a hurricane to form, a number of weather conditions must occur at the same time.

Tropical heat engines

A hurricane needs warm ocean water to form. The sun must heat the water to a temperature of at least 80° Fahrenheit (26.5° Celsius), and that water needs to be at least 200 feet (60 meters) deep in order for a hurricane to form. Warm ocean water will act as a fuel for a growing hurricane. Without this thick, warm layer of ocean water, the surrounding winds and **currents** will mix the warm water with colder water from below, and prevent a storm from occurring. Perfect ocean conditions only occur in parts of the world close to the **equator**, where the sun's rays heat the ocean water very strongly during the summer and early autumn.

Hurricanes help move warm air from the tropical parts of the Earth to its cooler parts. Evaporated ocean water provides rain to drier parts of the world. A quarter of Japan's rain comes from typhoons.

Condensation

As warm, moist air rises, it cools and forms **droplets** of water that turn into clouds. This process is called condensation. When rain falls from clouds, heat energy is released. The faster the rain falls the more energy is created, resulting in a thunderstorm. During the thunderstorm, warm air rises up in a column, cools off, and spreads out, making the storm cloud bigger.

Air pressure

When there is a mass of **high pressure** in the **atmosphere** above a growing storm, the air flows outward. Warm, moisture-filled air from the storm flows upward into these **low pressure** areas, and even more air rises. A hurricane's strong winds are caused by the air near the ocean's surface rushing in to replace air rising in the storm.

How ocean storms start

1. The sun's rays heat the ocean and cause the water to evaporate and become a gas, or water vapor.

2. Water vapor rises with warm air (red arrows), while cooler air (blue arrows) rushes in to replace it, creating wind.

3. Water vapor cools as it rises and condenses into clouds and rain.

4. As the cycle repeats itself, the energy released by condensation causes stronger winds to form. These stronger winds help to cause more warm air to rise and the storm grows.

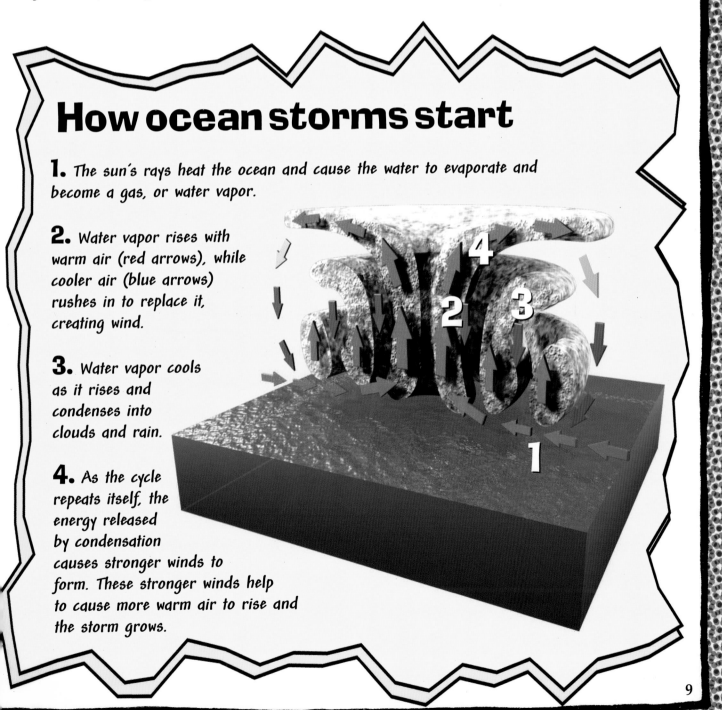

Wind systems

During the summer months, numerous tropical thunderstorms develop at the same time. Many of these thunderstorms form along the two wind belts located just north and south of the equator called the trade winds. The trade winds meet near the equator in an area of cloudy, rainy weather called the intertropical convergence zone. This is where many of the world's tropical thunderstorms develop.

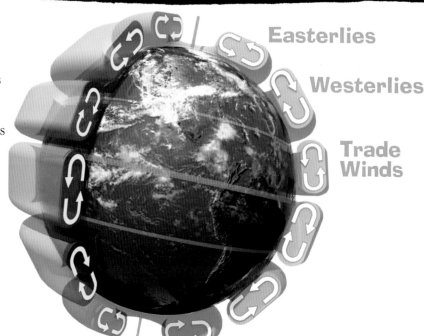

Easterlies

Westerlies

Trade Winds

Stages of a hurricane

Tropical disturbance

A tropical disturbance is the first stage of a hurricane's development. This occurs when thunder clouds gather into a cluster over tropical waters around a center of low pressure. Winds during a tropical disturbance move at less than 23 miles per hour (35 km/h).

Tropical depression

When the air pressure in a tropical disturbance continues to drop, the winds begin moving in a cyclonic, or swirling, pattern. Tropical depressions have surface wind speeds from 23 to 39 miles per hour (35 to 62 km/h). At this stage of development, swirling winds start to rotate around a center. This is known as "closed wind circulation."

Storm clusters gather

Winds rotate around a center

Coriolis effect

When thunderstorms gather together, they start to spin. At the same time, the force created by the spinning of the Earth causes the air inside the thunderstorm to travel in a spiral pattern. This is known as the Coriolis effect. The spin gives hurricanes **momentum**. In the northern **hemisphere,** hurricanes spin in a counterclockwise direction. In the southern hemisphere, they spin clockwise.

Inside the eye of a hurricane, clear blue skies are often visible.

Tropical storm

A tropical storm is just slightly weaker than a hurricane, and will develop into a hurricane if air conditions change. Tropical storms have swirling winds with speeds of 39 to 73 miles per hour (63 to 118 km/h). At this stage, tropical storms are given names.

The storm is given a name

Hurricane

When the winds of a tropical storm reach 74 miles per hour (120 km/h), it becomes a hurricane. The winds are organized around a well-defined center, called the eye. Many hurricanes are downgraded to tropical storms and tropical depressions as they move inland and become weaker.

Eye is clearly defined

Eye in the Sky

From above, a hurricane looks like an enormous doughnut, with a big hole in its middle and a lot of fluffy clouds forming its outer parts. The inside of a hurricane is a swirling mass of air and moisture.

Eye

At the center of every hurricane is a column, or tunnel, called the eye. In the eye, cool air (blue arrows) sinks back down to the ocean water below, collecting vapor along the way. Air and moisture swirl around outside while the eye remains clear and calm. Eyes can be 8 miles (12 km) to over 120 miles (200 km) across.

Eyewall

Just outside the eye, in the part of the hurricane known as the eyewall, are the hurricane's strongest and fastest winds. The winds spiral up to the top of the hurricane. This creates a state of low pressure, which allows more and more wind to be sucked into the hurricane. Winds exiting from inside the eyewall cool, and spin in the opposite direction.

Rim

At the outside of the huge mass of air, moisture, and clouds, the hurricane's force is weakest. In the rim of a hurricane, winds of up to 100 miles per hour (160 km/h) often bring huge amounts of rain.

Rainbands

Dozens of long, narrow bands of thunderstorms exist in every hurricane. These bands spiral counterclockwise in the northern hemisphere around the center of the storm. Warm, moist air (orange arrows) rises vertically from the ocean into the bands, and then descends as it cools (blue arrows) on either side of the band.

Storm surge

As a hurricane moves toward a coastline, the ocean starts to rise. This results in storm surge. It can flood communities and damage beaches. As a hurricane's winds spin around the eye, the low air pressure acts like suction in a straw, causing the water near the center of the storm to rise in a mound. The strong winds inside the hurricane act like a plow, allowing water to pile up. These two effects cause a large bulge of water to develop. Over deep water far from land, the water in the bulge flows away, keeping the rise in sea level small. Closer to shore, the build up of excess water has no place to go so it spills onto the coastline, flooding the beach.

eye

surge

Life of a Hurricane

Each hurricane region experiences a number of storms every year. In the Atlantic Ocean, six to eight hurricanes usually occur every year, while in the northern part of the Pacific, there are usually about 25 typhoons per year. In the southern Pacific, up to 15 cyclones occur annually.

HURRICANE HUGO
8 PM EDT
17 SEPTEMBER 1989
140 MPH   939 MB

Long lifespans

Hurricanes last longer and travel farther than other kinds of storms. From start to finish, a hurricane usually lasts between two and 14 days and travels as far as 4,000 miles (6,400 km). The longest lasting hurricane on record is Typhoon John, which raged over the Pacific Ocean for 31 days in 1994.

In 1989, Hurricane Hugo began as a tropical storm off the coast of western Africa, crossed the Atlantic Ocean, and smashed into the Caribbean islands of Guadeloupe and Antigua, before devastating Puerto Rico, the Virgin Islands, and large chunks of the United States mainland. Hugo lasted 12 days.

Going with the flow

A hurricane moves forward in a straight path, zigs and zags or loops around, or barely moves at all. Most hurricanes follow westward paths and curve north or south depending on which hemisphere they form in. Atlantic hurricanes are blown westward by trade winds, which take them across the Caribbean Sea and the Gulf of Mexico, where they turn north before reaching land. In the north Pacific Ocean, typhoons also travel west. Indian Ocean cyclones generally travel north. On average, hurricanes travel at speeds between ten and twenty miles per hour (16 and 32 km/h).

Making landfall

Hurricanes remain powerful while they travel over tropical waters. Most hurricanes die off while passing over cooler ocean waters before they ever reach land. Those that do make landfall quickly die as cooler air and lack of moisture over land cut off their energy source. Even at less than their full strength, hurricanes can still cause tremendous damage once they make landfall and move inland. Ninety percent of the deaths associated with a hurricane occur when it hits land. Hurricanes that curve away from land sometimes become **extratropical** cyclones, and cause havoc for ships.

The Name Game

Scientists name hurricanes and tropical storms. Before 1950, hurricanes were simply referred to by their dates and locations. This system was confusing because there were sometimes more than one hurricane in the same place at the same time. To make identification clearer, the World Meteorological Organization (WMO) began giving women's names to hurricanes in 1952, and in 1979, they started using male names as well. Now, the WMO alternates between male and female names for hurricanes, using a pre-set alphabetical list. Different sets of names are used for hurricanes in the Atlantic and Pacific regions, and they are repeated every six years. Typhoons in the Pacific region did not receive names until 2000. Typhoon names usually refer to animals, astrological signs, and people's names.

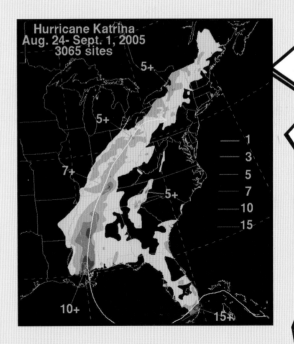

(left) Very destructive hurricanes, such as Katrina in 2005, have their names "retired." This means that the name cannot be used again.

The Coming Storm

Millions of people around the world make their homes in places where the threat of hurricanes and typhoons is part of daily life. People have tried for centuries to predict when these storms were coming and where they would strike. Today, advances in technology have made it possible to predict the behavior of hurricanes with a high degree of accuracy.

Cloud seeding

No one has figured out a way to prevent hurricanes from forming, but scientists in the United States tried during the 1970s. Airplanes would fly over storm clouds and drop the chemical silver iodide into them in a process called "cloud seeding." Scientists hoped the silver iodide would cause water in the clouds to turn to ice crystals that would either melt into rain or fall as snow, instead of forming into a hurricane. Cloud seeding was not successful.

(top) Hurricane specialists at the National Hurricane Center keep a close watch on Hurricane Ivan and inform people of its path.

(bottom) Computers at the National Hurricane Center capture and analyze information about how a hurricane is going to behave.

This picture is of a satellite image of Hurricane Ike, which began as a tropical storm near the Cape Verde islands, in the central Atlantic Ocean. By studying satellite images, meteorologists were able to detect an eye beginning to form in the center of the cyclone on September, 3, 2008. The storm was upgraded to a hurricane, which strengthened to a Category 4 with maximum sustained winds of 145 miles per hour (230 km/h).

National Hurricane Center

In the United States, the Miami, Florida-based National Hurricane Center (NHC) employs a team of experienced meteorologists. Using the latest hurricane-forecasting equipment, meteorologists attempt to learn more about hurricanes, and to save lives through accurate predictions and warnings about the arrival of these storms.

Satellites and radar

Meteorologists use satellite images and radar to **track** storms. Satellites 20,000 miles (32,000 km) above the Earth take pictures of hurricane clouds and send them back to meteorologists to study. Radar systems bounce **radio waves** off moisture droplets within hurricane clouds to form an accurate picture of the size and speed of the storm. As advanced as satellites and radar tracking have become, they are not always accurate.

(above) Hurricane Hunters fly specially equipped airplanes through the eyes of hurricanes to gather information about their wind speed and direction. The Hurricane Hunters pass this information on to the NHC, which issues warnings to people in the hurricane's path.

Path of Destruction

Hurricanes kill more people than all other kinds of storms combined. Wherever a hurricane makes landfall, there is a chance its high winds, rain, and storm surge will cause terrible destruction and death.

Blown away

Very powerful hurricanes have wind speeds that approach 200 miles per hour (320 km/h). Fierce winds uproot trees, telephone poles, and other structures that are not firmly attached to the ground. A hurricane's strong winds also rip the roofs off houses, blow cars and mobile homes through the air, and smash ships at sea. In cities, winds lift up signs, outdoor furniture, and bicycles and shoot them through the air, where they become hazardous **projectiles**.

(below) When Hurricane Camille hit the United States mainland in 1969, its vicious winds of nearly 200 miles per hour (320 km/h) flattened homes and left 250 people dead and many thousands homeless.

Rain, floods, and mudslides

The amount of rain dumped by a hurricane can lead to **flash floods** and mudslides. During the landfall of a typical hurricane in the United States, about 10 to 15 inches (35 to 43 cm) of rain falls. If a hurricane is large and moving slowly, the rain is not absorbed into the ground fast enough, and overflows rivers and streams, leading to severe flooding. In Bangladesh, a country located just east of India, nearly ten million people lost their homes because of flooding during a 1991 cyclone. In South and Central America, hillside rocks, trees, and dirt are loosened by a hurricane's rain, leading to massive mudslides that wipe out entire villages.

(right) Some areas of Honduras received as much as 75 inches (190 cm) of rain during Hurricane Mitch in 1998. This led to mudslides throughout the country.

Flash floods caused by a hurricane's rain can occur very quickly. This man in Brownsville, Texas, pushes his stalled car through a flooded street after Hurricane Dolly.

Storm surge

The surge of ocean water that smashes into land when a hurricane makes landfall is the greatest danger to human life and property. When the storm surge combines with normal tides, it increases water levels by fifteen feet (4.5 meters) or more and leads to widespread flooding. In many parts of the United States, **densely** populated coastal areas along the Atlantic and Gulf coasts are less than ten feet (three meters) above **sea level**, making them even more vulnerable to increased water levels. The most destructive storm surge to hit the United States occurred during Hurricane Camille in 1969. The waters along the Mississippi coast rose 24 feet (seven meters) and swept away bridges, buildings, and trees. In Australia, the Bathurst Bay Hurricane of 1899 had the highest storm surge ever recorded, with a wall of water 42 feet (13 meters) high.

(above) High winds increase the size of waves on top of the storm surge.

(left) The storm surge during the 1900 hurricane that hit Galveston, Texas, quickly pushed water levels to 15 feet (5 meters) high in the streets. 3,000 homes were destroyed and 8,000 people died.

Tornadoes

Violent swirling windstorms, known as tornadoes, can occur when a hurricane reaches land. Most North American hurricanes create at least a single tornado, usually in its rainband area. Tornadoes caused by hurricanes are rarely accompanied by hail or much lightning, but their strong winds can cause significant damage.

In 1967, Hurricane Beulah reportedly set off 141 tornadoes across Texas.

Saffir-Simpson Scale

In the 1970s, two American scientists, Herbert S. Saffir and Robert H. Simpson, developed a system for rating the strength of hurricanes. The Saffir-Simpson scale contains five categories based on factors such as the speed of the winds within the hurricane and the height of its storm surge. Hurricanes rated as Category 1 are the weakest, while Category 5 hurricanes are the most destructive.

Hurricane Effects

	Wind	Storm Surge	Results
Category 1	74-95 mph (119-153 km/h)	4-5 feet (1.2-1.5 m)	Damaged trees; flooding of coastal roads
Category 2	96-110 mph (154-177 km/h)	6-8 feet (1.8-2.4 m)	Damaged trees, roofs, windows; homes near coast destroyed
Category 3	111-129 mph (178-208 km/h)	9-12 feet (2.7-3.6 m)	Extensive flooding near coasts; serious damage to mobile and permanent homes
Category 4	130-154 mph (209-248 km/h)	13-18 feet (3.9-5.4 m)	Possible total damage of homes; extensive flooding up to five miles (10 km) inland
Category 5	More than 154 mph (More than 248 km/h)	18 feet and higher (5.4 m and higher)	Total destruction of buildings; flooding up to ten miles (16 km) inland

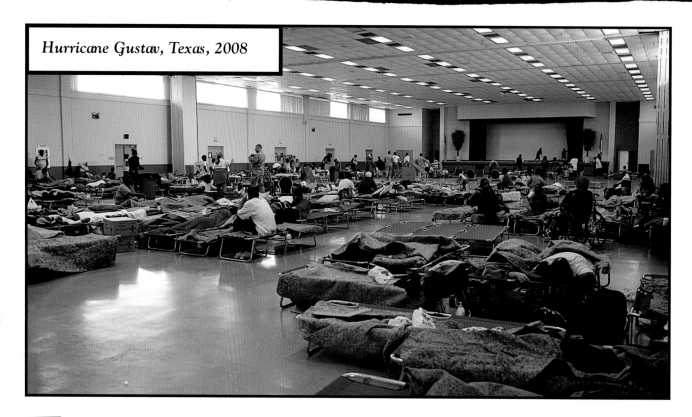

Famous Hurricanes

Hurricanes, like other disasters, have occurred throughout history. Not much information about hurricanes is available before the 1800s, when official records started to be kept on the loss of human life and property damage. Since then, many hurricanes have become well-known because of their destruction.

Hurricane Katrina

After forming over the Bahamas on August 23, 2005, Hurricane Katrina swept across southern Florida. As it traveled over the Gulf of Mexico, Katrina became a Category 5 hurricane with winds reaching 175 miles per hour (280 km/h) before making its final landfall as a Category 3 hurricane near the mouth of the Pearl River in Louisiana six days later. The hurricane's storm surge and the heavy rainfall that it brought caused 53 levees to break in New Orleans, flooding the city. More than 1,800 people died in the hurricane and the floods, making Hurricane Katrina the deadliest hurricane in the United States since the 1928 Okeechobee Hurricane.

(above) Evacuees fleeing Hurricane Gustav take shelter in a convention center in Texas. Gustav caused the largest evacuation in United States history, forcing three million people to leave their homes. Gustav hit Haiti, the Dominican Republic, Jamaica, the Cayman Islands, Cuba, and the United States, causing at least $6.6 billion in damages.

Cyclone Nargis

On May 2, 2008, the tropical cyclone Nargis made landfall in the Ayeyarwady region of Burma after reaching peak winds of 135 miles per hour (215 km/h). It developed nine days earlier in the central area of the Bay of Bengal. Cyclone Nargis was one of the deadliest cyclones in the North Indian Ocean basin, killing at least 138,000 people. Yangon, Burma's largest city, was ravaged, as was the Irrawaddy Delta, where most of the country's rice cultivation took place.

Bangladesh cyclones

Northeast of India, in the country of Bangladesh, the Ganges River empties into the Bay of Bengal. Cyclones that form in the Indian Ocean move north to Bangladesh and have catastrophic results. A cyclone in 1970 caused massive flooding and **famine** and led to the death of an estimated 500,000 people. In 1985, another cyclone killed 11,000 people.

Typhoon Mireille

In 1991, Typhoon Mireille became one of the costliest natural disasters in northern Pacific history. Damages were nearly eight billion dollars by the end of the 72-hour storm, and 54 lives were lost, including a Korean ship's entire crew.

Orissa, India, 1999

Hurricane Ike, Texas, 2008

(above) A starving boy eats a few pieces of grain. In 1999, a "super cyclone" battered the Orissa region of India for 36 hours. The cyclone's 190 mile per hour (300 km/h) winds and 30-foot (ten-meter) storm surge, led to the death of 20,000 people. Millions were left homeless and hungry.

(left) Hurricane Ike was the third costliest hurricane in U.S. history, only surpassed by Andrew in 1992 and Katrina in 2005.

Hurricane Safety

Even though it is now possible for scientists to predict when a hurricane will reach land and how powerful it will be, it is still important to take precautions. Communities where hurricanes are common develop systems of warnings and plans to keep people and property safe.

Watches and warnings

The National Hurricane Center in the United States provides two forms of advance notice of the arrival of hurricanes. A "hurricane watch" is issued when it looks like a hurricane will make landfall within 24 to 36 hours. The message is spread by radio and TV to people in the area, but forecasters usually do not know exactly how wide an area will be covered, or what exact location will be hit the hardest. A "hurricane warning" is issued when a specific area is identified. People living in the area are warned they may have to **evacuate**, or leave their homes. Most communities in high-risk areas have emergency and evacuation plans.

High winds can hurl debris through the air and break windows, resulting in cuts and other injuries to people. Boarding up windows or putting storm shutters and tape on windows prevents glass from shattering.

Cyclone shelters

In densely-populated Bangladesh, flooding caused by cyclones results in many deaths. The Bangladesh government has been working to develop a system of cyclone shelters. About 1,350 of these shelters offer safety to about 1.3 million people when cyclones hit. The construction of cyclone shelters in Bangladesh is ongoing, but the shelters do not entirely solve the problem of safety during a large cyclone. A forecasting network is being developed to more accurately predict cyclones and get the information to people in high-risk areas.

Cyclone shelters protect more than one million people in Bangladesh, while another 2.3 million people can take shelter in other buildings. Another eleven million people are left with no real safe place during a cyclone.

Family disaster plans

Prediction methods help people know when hurricanes are coming, but it is also important to know how to prepare for its arrival. In the United States, the Federal Emergency Management Administration recommends developing a Family Disaster Plan to prepare for hurricanes.

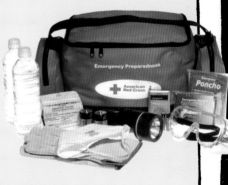

The Plan includes the following safety tips:

- Keep a battery-powered radio on hand to listen to news about the hurricane
- Have "disaster supplies" on hand, such as a first-aid kit, food, and water
    - Keep emergency numbers by the phone for easy access
    - Make sure an adult turns off all utilities in the house
    - Have a meeting place in your neighborhood for family members
    - Have a family member who lives outside of the area directly affected by the hurricane act as a phone contact for family members who get separated

FIRST AID

Surviving the Storm

Life is never the same again for people who survive a hurricane. Friends, family, and pets may have been killed or seriously injured, and the roads, buildings, and recreation areas of entire communities may have been swept away in an instant. Homes and possessions, such as cars, furniture, appliances, along with children's toys, often will have been destroyed in the storm as well.

Starting over again

In many areas, such as the southeastern part of the United States, hurricanes hit places where people are not wealthy. Some people there live in small houses or trailers, and many do not have any **insurance** on their homes or possessions. For these people, hurricane damage means starting all over again.

(above) Houses are instantly turned to rubble, leaving many people with nowhere to live.

Short-term housing

Most areas that are vulnerable to hurricanes have a plan in place for dealing with the aftermath. In the United States, the federal government and state and local governments work with organizations such as the Red Cross, to establish hurricane evacuation plans. Often, the military also gets involved to help people recover from the disaster. They build "tent cities" to provide shelter, hand out food and water, and hook up generators to supply electrical power.

(above) Relief organizations build "tent cities" to shelter those left homeless by hurricanes and other disasters.

Environment

Many hurricanes completely destroy forests, eliminating huge supplies of lumber and destroying the homes of thousands of animals. Freshwater streams and rivers can also be **contaminated** by the debris that falls into them during a hurricane. In many parts of the world, drinking water contamination causes serious health risks for people.

Agriculture and marine life

Agricultural land can be seriously damaged in a hurricane. Flooding causes the **erosion** of soil that is needed to grow crops for food. In parts of the world where farming is important for human and animal survival, this causes great problems. Marine life is also affected by hurricanes. Hurricanes often wipe out thousands of fish and cause many people in the fishing industry to lose their jobs.

(above) Volunteers in New Orleans, Louisiana, help distribute food and necessities to people affected by Hurricane Katrina.

Famine

Following Hurricane Mitch in 1998, more than one million people in agricultural areas of Central America, especially in Honduras and Nicaragua, experienced severe famine because their crops and farms were destroyed. International relief programs brought food for people to eat for several years afterward. Countries from around the world sent supplies, workers, and funds to help the people of these devastated nations. Also in 1998, after cyclones caused enormous floods in coastal Bangladesh, relief agencies supplied food to an estimated five million people facing starvation.

After Effects

When a hurricane hits a heavily-populated area, the effects can be devastating. Billions of dollars in property damage means there is always a lot of work to be done after the hurricane. Many people who have lost their homes need to be rescued and re-located to safer places.

Lessons learned

The lessons that are learned in areas hit hard by hurricanes help to prevent damage in future storms. When rebuilding structures that have been damaged by a hurricane, construction crews often add reinforcements to foundations and walls that can prevent or reduce destruction if a hurricane hits again.

People in countries where cyclones and typhoons are common have ways of reducing the damage these storms cause. In Bangladesh, people build huge barriers out of rock to stem the floods that occur during cyclones. In other parts of the world, people construct their houses on stilts to prevent damage from flooding.

When Hurricane Hugo finished its devastating run in 1989, it was estimated that the amount of lumber destroyed in forests was enough to build 300,000 houses!

(left) After a hurricane, it may take days, weeks, or even months to restore power. Electrical crews from many states, including this crew from Arizona, came to Texas to help restore power after Hurricane Ike.

Galveston seawall

During the 1900 hurricane that hit Galveston, Texas, high winds and waves built a barrier of wreckage that jammed up against the shoreline, protecting some buildings and people behind it. To protect themselves from future hurricane damage, the residents of Galveston built a proper seawall. In 1915, another powerful hurricane hit Galveston and the seawall saved many lives.

Cleanup

In the United States, the Federal Emergency Management Agency (FEMA) cleans up and assists people after any large disaster. FEMA works with local companies, to build temporary shelters for people and animals, provide food and water for those who have lost their homes, and set up communications centers for communities that have lost electricity and phone lines.

Typhoon Defense

Typhoons cause deadly flooding in Japan. In the city of Osaka, city planners built a series of floodgates on major rivers to prevent water from building up and rushing into the city during future typhoons. Under normal circumstances, water flows under these gates, but when a typhoon arrives, bringing with it increased water levels, the gates immediately flip over and prevent the high tides from flooding the areas near the rivers.

Recipe for Disaster

Here is a fun and simple activity you can do at home to understand the movement of strong winds and rain during a hurricane.

What you need:
* A large bowl, tub, or basin (made of glass or Pyrex, if possible)
* A large mixing spoon or ruler
* Food coloring

What to do:
1. Fill the tub, bowl, or basin about half full with water.

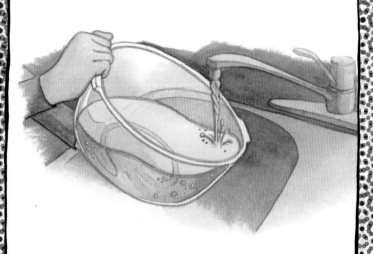

2. With the ruler or spoon, stir the water in a counterclockwise circular motion. Increase the speed of your stirring a little at a time.

3. As you stir faster and faster, a "hole" free of water should develop in the middle. This is similar to what happens when the "eye" develops in the middle of a hurricane.

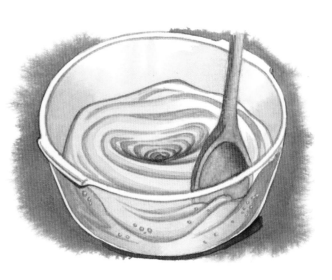

4. While you are stirring, add some food coloring and then stop stirring. The color should move out away from the center, and into the water that is swirling around the outside.

What you will see:
These bands of color are similar to the clouds that form outside the hurricane's eye.

Glossary

atmosphere A huge blanket of gases that surround the Earth

contaminate To pollute

current Paths or flows

dense Packed closely together

droplets Tiny drops

equator The imaginary line around the middle of the Earth

erosion The process of being worn away, as by water and wind

evacuation The act of leaving an area or building

extratropical Occurring outside the tropics

famine A lack of available food

flash flood A surge of water that occurs very quickly during a rainstorm

hemisphere The halves into which the Earth is divided

high pressure An air mass that usually creates clear and dry weather

insurance An amount of money paid for loss or damage in exchange for regular payments

low pressure An air mass that usually creates cloudy and rainy weather

meteorologist A person who studies all aspects of the weather

momentum The force or speed of an object in motion

projectile An object that is shot or thrown through the air

radio waves Energy waves that carry signals between points without using wires

sea level The level of the surface of the ocean

shaman Someone who practices healing

track To follow the movement of something

Index

Websites

Get all your hurricane questions answered at:
www.weatherwizkids.com/weather-hurricane.htm

Find out more about how hurricanes form and what to do if one is approaching at:
www.skydiary.com/kids/hurricanes.html